MORRIS AUTOMATED INFORMATION NETWORK

0 1029 0682170 1

Parsippany-Troy Hills Library
Main Library
449 Halsey RD
Parsippany NJ 07054
973-887-5150

NOV 1 8 2016

D1716654

WITHDRAWN

SOLE SURVIVOR

SURVIVING THE DESERT

Louise Spilsbury

Gareth Stevens
PUBLISHING

Please visit our website, www.garethstevens.com.
For a free color catalog of all our high-quality books,
call toll free 1-800-542-2595 or fax 1-877-542-2596.

CATALOGING-IN-PUBLICATION DATA

Names: Spilsbury, Louise.
Title: Surviving the desert / Louise Spilsbury.
Description: New York : Gareth Stevens Publishing, 2017. | Series: Sole survivor |
    Includes index.
Identifiers: ISBN 9781482450910 (pbk.) | ISBN 9781482450934 (library bound) |
    ISBN 9781482450927 (6 pack)
Subjects: LCSH: Desert survival--Juvenile literature.
Classification: LCC GV200.5 S65 2017 | DDC 613.6'9--dc23

First Edition

Published in 2017 by
Gareth Stevens Publishing
111 East 14th Street, Suite 349
New York, NY 10003

© 2017 Gareth Stevens Publishing

Produced for Gareth Stevens by Calcium
Editors: Sarah Eason and Jennifer Sanderson
Designer: Paul Myerscough

Picture credits: Cover: Shutterstock: Andrey Armyagov (left), Tom Reichner
(right). Inside: Shutterstock: Johnny Adolphson 14–15, Galyna Andrushko 20,
Bikeriderlondon 20–21, 36–37, Gualtiero Boffi 11, Deviant 32, Katie Dickinson
6–7, Anton Foltin 5, Dejan Gileski 28, Iofoto 37, Marques 4–5, 12–13, Stephen
Mcsweeny 1, 24–25, Paul B. Moore 28–29, Tyler Olson 41, Jay Ondreicka 22–23,
Marco Ossino 18–19, PatriciaDz 32–33, Sergey Pesterev 10–11, Maxim Petrichuk
30–31, Styve Reineck 9, Richard Lightscapes 40–41, Mark Skalny 14, 42–43,
Aliaksei Smalenski 8–9, Solis Images 38–39, Calin Tatu 34–35, Tidarat Tiemjai 17,
Kris Wiktor 16–17, 26–27.

All rights reserved. No part of this book may be reproduced in any form
without permission from the publisher, except by reviewer.

Printed in the United States of America
CPSIA compliance information: Batch #CS16GS:
For further information contact Gareth Stevens, New York, New York at 1-800-542-2595.

CONTENTS

Chapter One

DESERT DANGERS

Deserts are amazing places, but these sandy, rocky wildernesses can also be deadly. Some deserts are so hot during the day that most rain that falls is quickly lost through **evaporation**.

Deserts get fewer than 10 inches (250 mm) of rain a year, and many get a lot less than that. The heat is severe, but at night it can become freezing cold, too. The combination of extreme temperatures, high winds, and rough land can damage vehicles and leave people stranded in the desert.

Hot, dry deserts cover about one-fifth of Earth's surface.

Some deserts are so dry they have few plants. Others, like this one, get enough rain for some plants to grow.

Perfect Planning

To survive desert dangers, people must be well-prepared.
One of the most important things is to plan a desert trip in advance.
Those traveling to deserts must understand the possible dangers.
To survive, there are some basic rules everyone should follow:

- Always carry an emergency kit containing water and food.
- Wear suitable clothing for protection against the extreme weather.
- Pack a **global positioning system (GPS)** device and a **satellite phone**.
- People should tell friends and family where they plan to go and when they are due back. If they get lost or are in trouble, someone will know something is wrong when they do not return on time.

In this book we are going to look at some of the hazards people face in deserts, and how some people have survived the most terrifying dangers of all.

Read each page carefully—there are a lot of survival tips and some great information that will help you correctly answer the Do or Die questions. You can find the answers on pages 44 and 45.

SEEKING SHADE

Daytime desert heat can be a killer. The Sahara is the biggest desert in the world and one of the hottest places on Earth. There, it can regularly be as hot as 122 degrees Fahrenheit (50 °C) in spring and summer. If a person's temperature rises too high and they do not take measures to cool down, the body can lose its ability to cool down and control its temperature. This is **heatstroke** and it can damage the brain and other **internal organs**.

People who get heatstroke suffer painful headaches. They feel dizzy and sick, and may vomit. Their muscles start to twitch and they may also become confused. Sometimes, they may start to hallucinate—to see things that are not there. Eventually, they lose consciousness. As soon as people get any heatstroke **symptoms**, they should find shade, lie down with their feet raised, loosen their clothing, and drink water.

"I SURVIVED..."

SHANNON FRASER, A WOMAN FROM NORTH QUEENSLAND, AUSTRALIA, WENT INTO THE DESERT PLANNING TO GO FOR A SWIM AT A WATERING HOLE. UNFORTUNATELY, SHE GOT LOST AND WANDERED IN THE DESERT FOR ALMOST TWO WEEKS. SHE HAD LITTLE CLOTHING WITH HER, SO BY THE TIME SHE STUMBLED INTO A PARKING LOT AND GOT HELP, SHE HAD SEVERE SUNBURN FROM BEING EXPOSED TO THE SUN EVERY DAY.

Reducing the Risk

There are things people can do to reduce the risk of heatstroke:

- Drink plenty of water.
- Reduce sweating (which is water loss) by resting often in shade.
- Walk early or later in the day to avoid the heat.
- Walk in the shade of mountains or overhanging rocks that block any direct sunlight.

It is wise for walkers to take advantage of any shade they can find to bring some relief from the daytime heat.

Do or Die

Your jeep breaks down in the desert and you have a long walk back to the nearest town. To avoid heatstroke, do you:

a Walk during the day and rest at night?

b Walk during the morning and evening and seek shade in the hottest part of the day?

c Walk day and night to get back to safety as quickly as you can?

SUNBURN

When it is hot, people usually like to wear shorts and T-shirts, but this is not a good idea in the desert. There is little shade in a desert. The sun's **ultraviolet (UV)** rays shine on people and also **reflect** off the sand, hitting the skin twice. Strong sunlight can cause severe and painful sunburn, and the sun's rays can burn skin, even when it does not seem bright. Severe sunburn can be fatal.

Clothing can protect the skin from the sun's dangerous rays. Wearing long, loose clothing is best, because this covers the skin and allows air to circulate under the garments to keep people cool. In extreme environments like deserts, where the sun is strongest, its best to wear long-sleeve tops and long pants made from special fabric that has UV protection.

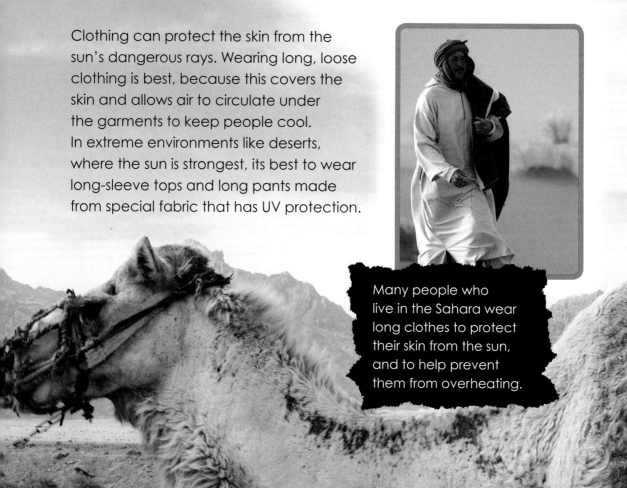

Many people who live in the Sahara wear long clothes to protect their skin from the sun, and to help prevent them from overheating.

Color Codes

Light colors reflect the sun's rays and dark colors absorb them. That is why, in the desert, it is best to wear thin, lightweight, and light-colored clothes to help keep down the body temperature. Unusually, some Bedouin people who live in the deserts of Africa wear thick black robes. The outer black robe does absorb heat, but the heat is not passed onto the body because the fabric is so thick.

Eye Protection

To protect the head, neck, and face, people should wear a hat with a wide brim. It is also very important to wear sunglasses to protect the eyes, even on cloudy days. The sun is so bright it may cause long-term damage. If people lose their sunglasses, they should protect their eyes by making a sun shield from cardboard, cloth, a hat, or a scarf.

In the desert, people should wear sunblock on any parts of their skin that are not covered by clothes.

Do or Die

You are planning a hike in a desert and are choosing what clothes to wear. Do you choose:

a Thin, light-colored, loose long pants and a long-sleeve shirt?

b Thin, dark-colored tight clothes?

c A T-shirt and shorts?

Chapter Two

SHELTER

Heat is one of the biggest daytime desert dangers, but at night there is a greater risk of getting too cold in the desert. While temperatures can soar to more than 120 degrees Fahrenheit (49 °C) in the day, evening temperatures can fall to just above freezing. It is important to try to stay as warm as possible at night. Without shelter or some means of keeping warm, **hypothermia** is a real risk.

When you are awake, the core (center) of your body needs to stay at a steady temperature of about 98.6 degrees Fahrenheit (37 °C) to work properly. When it is very cold, your body loses heat to its surroundings. If the body gets too cold, it starts to shut down, and, eventually, vital organs stop working. This is known as hypothermia and it can be deadly.

Nights are cold in a desert because there are no clouds to trap the heat, so it escapes into space.

Signs and Symptoms

People should watch out for any of the following symptoms of hypothermia and try to warm up as soon as they can:

- Shivering, cold, pale, and dry skin
- Tiredness, confusion, and odd behavior
- Slow and shallow breathing
- Slow and weakening **pulse**

Vehicle Shelter

If people are driving through the desert and their vehicle breaks down, the best thing they can do is to stay in their vehicle. Not only does this make people easier to find, for example, if a helicopter is searching for them, but it also means they have somewhere to shelter. If they get inside the vehicle at night and close all the windows and doors, the vehicle will give them some protection from the cold.

Do or Die

It is late afternoon and your vehicle breaks down while you are driving across a wide, empty section of desert. Do you:

a Leave the vehicle and walk to find help?

b Stay inside the vehicle to keep warm?

c Sit outside the vehicle at night to keep a lookout for rescuers?

MAKING SHELTERS

People make shelters to survive the heat during the day and the cold at night in the desert. When planning an overnight trip to a desert that gets cold at night, people should pack a tent and a good goose-down sleeping bag. If they are stranded in the desert, they can make a shelter to protect themselves from the sun and cold, but they should build it in a cool time of the day to avoid **heat exhaustion**.

People can build a shelter by piling up rocks to build walls that keep out the wind. Then, they can drape a sheet over the top of the walls to make a daytime shelter. At night, they can hang the sheet from one wall and weigh it down around themselves to keep warm. In sandy deserts, a ditch with sticks holding up a sheet roof keeps out sunlight, and at night the ditch can provide warmth.

"I SURVIVED..."

When 59-year-old Victoria Grover jumped off a ledge and broke her leg during a hike in the Utah desert in 2012, she could not walk. She had not told anyone where she was going, had no food, and faced freezing nighttime temperatures. She survived by sleeping during the day and staying awake all night, wrapping herself in a poncho to break the wind, and by burning scraps of wood. She was found on her fourth day, suffering from hypothermia.

Making Fires

Making a fire will help keep people warm, but it can be difficult to find wood in the desert. Away from watering holes, deserts are too hot and dry for many trees to survive, so mainly **scrub** and grasses grow there. Dry grasses are useful for starting a fire if people can also find wood to burn and keep the fire going.

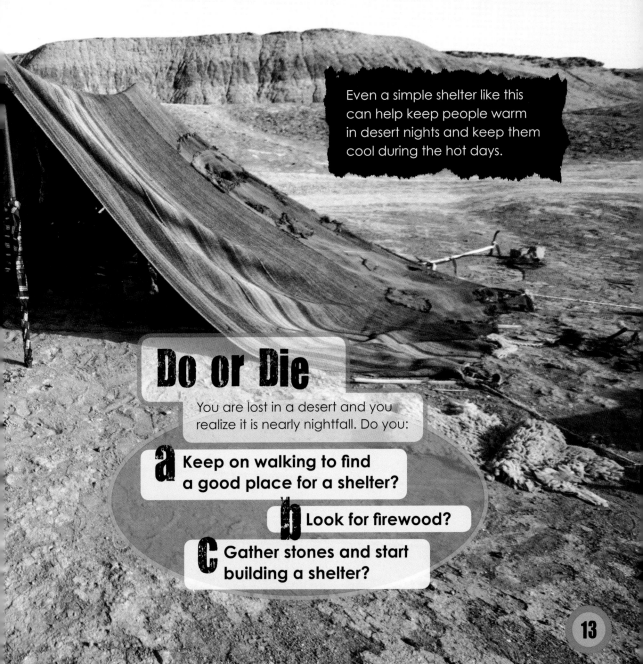

Even a simple shelter like this can help keep people warm in desert nights and keep them cool during the hot days.

Do or Die

You are lost in a desert and you realize it is nearly nightfall. Do you:

a Keep on walking to find a good place for a shelter?

b Look for firewood?

c Gather stones and start building a shelter?

Chapter Three

FOOD AND DRINK

Most visitors to the desert take their own supplies of food and water. This is because it can be difficult to find supplies in deserts. The extremes of temperature and lack of water make it difficult for many plants to survive. With fewer plants, there is less food for animals to eat, so there are fewer animals, too.

Some plants are **adapted** to survive in the desert. People cannot eat their leaves because many desert plants have few or no leaves. Many desert plants, like cacti, have spines instead of leaves. Plants lose water through their leaves, but spines hold on to water. Other plants are not available to eat for most of the year, because they stay **dormant** under the ground in hot, dry times and grow only in the rainy season.

Desert hikers should carry a supply of food like high-energy snacks so they do not go hungry.

Foods to Pack

When choosing meals for desert trips, people should avoid food that rots quickly in hot conditions and food that melts easily, such as chocolate. They should pack **carbohydrates**, such as bread or grains, because they provide a lot of energy. People should also carry foods that require little or no water to prepare, such as noodle cups and energy bars. They should also bring matches and a pot to cook food and heat water.

Do or Die

You are packing food for a desert hike with friends. What do you take in your backpack? Do you pack:

a High-energy foods such as bread and energy bars?

b Lots of chocolate?

c Just fresh fruit and vegetables?

Some deserts have enough dead and dry plants that people can use to build a fire on which they can cook food.

Salt

If people go on a hike that is particularly difficult or lasts for more than a few hours, they sweat a lot and lose salts from their body. These must be replaced or there is an increased risk of heatstroke. Salts can be replaced by eating food or chewing on salty snacks, such as beef jerky.

GETTING WATER

The human body is made up of three-quarters water, and it needs its balance of water to work properly. When people sweat, they lose water. In a very hot desert, people can lose about 1 pint (500 mm) of water an hour in sweat, even when they are sitting still. If people do not replace the fluids they lose through sweat, they are in danger of becoming **dehydrated** and this can be very dangerous.

Dehydration is a serious condition that occurs when more water leaves a body than is taken in. As well as feeling very thirsty, victims may feel dizzy and very tired. They may get a headache and a dry mouth, lips, and eyes. As dehydration becomes worse, people lose their strength, and gradually their body starts to shut down, unless they replace their fluids quickly.

Drink Up!

When going to a desert, people should always bring more water than they think they will need. They should also drink often and more than they think they need to. Sipping water to make it last is not a good idea—people have been found dead from dehydration with water still in their bottles. It is better to take a good drink often.

Do or Die

You are trekking in the desert during the day. You do not feel at all thirsty. Do you:

a Take small sips of water?

b Save your water for when you feel really thirsty?

c Force yourself to drink a good amount often?

Cacti Juice

If people run out of water, they may be able to find a watering hole or spring. To find one, they can look for birds in the morning and evening, because birds often circle water at these times. They can cut open cacti stems. Cacti store water in their stems, so people can suck juice from these plants and drink it.

Inside the leaves of the aloe vera plant is a gel that is a complete food and drink.

People should drink water only from sources that they are certain are clean and free from substances that can cause disease.

FINDING FOOD

When people get very hot, they usually do not feel like eating. This is not a bad thing, because eating uses water to help digest food. A human can survive more than three weeks without food, but they can survive only three to four days without water. If water is scarce, it is better to eat only small amounts of food, and try to eat foods that contain a lot of moisture, such as fruits and vegetables.

If people's food supplies run out, in an emergency, there are some wild foods they can eat. Most cacti fruits are edible, such as the fruit of the saguaro cactus and the prickly pear cactus. People can eat three parts of the prickly pear plant: the pad of the cactus can be eaten like a vegetable, the pear can be eaten like a fruit, and the petals of the flowers can be eaten, too.

Before visiting a desert region, it is a good idea to learn which plants can be eaten and which are poisonous.

"I SURVIVED..."

WHEN 28-YEAR-OLD WILLIAM LAFEVER WENT WALKING IN THE ESCALANTE DESERT IN UTAH, HE LOST HIS WAY. OVER THE NEXT THREE WEEKS, HE TRIED TO FIND HIS WAY, AND SURVIVED BY EATING ANYTHING EDIBLE HE COULD FIND, INCLUDING ROOTS AND FROGS. HE DRANK WATER FROM A RIVER. WHEN HE FINALLY SPOTTED A HELICOPTER, HE WAS SO WEAK HE COULD HARDLY LIFT HIS ARM TO WAVE TO IT.

Meaty Meals

If people find areas with plants, they may also be able to find and eat animals that live or shelter among the plants. These include ants and centipedes, birds, snakes, and desert rabbits or other small **mammals**. It is best to cook meat first in case it contains **bacteria** that can make people sick.

Do or Die

You are lost in a desert. You are tired and you do not have much food left. Do you:

a Stop eating?

b Eat all the food you have left?

c Eat small amounts of food?

Chapter Four

ANIMAL ATTACKS

Many dangerous desert animals lurk under the ground and under rocks. Some desert animals are gentle plant eaters. For example, gerbils scurry out from under rocks to find plant parts, such as seeds, which provide them with both the water and food they need. Other animals are **predators** that eat other animals. Predators can be dangerous to humans if they use their weapons, such as stingers, or bite them.

Insects, such as locusts, have hard, horny mouthparts to help them chew tough desert leaves. Ants are a nuisance because their bites can cause severe **allergic reactions**. These reactions can include blocked airways, making it very difficult to breathe. When people are so far from the hospital, allergic reactions like this can be very dangerous and, sometimes, fatal.

Desert hikers should watch where they walk to avoid disturbing an animal that might attack.

Take Precautions

Most animals will attack only if they feel threatened, so people can avoid danger by not touching or scaring the wildlife. People should never walk barefoot in the desert. The ground will burn their feet and animals under rocks will bite or sting the people who walk on them.

Avoiding Insects

Desert travelers should avoid nests or thick areas of grass where insects shelter and feed. People should also keep their shirts tucked into their pants and their pants tucked into their socks, to keep the skin protected. When they go to sleep, they should try to keep as much of their body covered and off the ground as possible.

Desert locusts travel in groups of millions and can devour all the edible plants in an area in minutes.

Do or Die

You are hiking in the desert and you spot an insect that looks interesting. You do not know what it is. Do you:

a Walk away from it?

b Go closer to it to investigate?

c Pick it up?

SCORPIONS

Scorpions are deadly desert predators. They have several **adaptations** that help them survive the heat and lack of water in the desert. They get water from the animals they eat. These include insects, spiders, other scorpions, and lizards. They have an exoskeleton (outer covering) that reduces the amount of water they lose through their skin. To avoid the heat, most scorpions rest in an underground burrow during the day and hunt at night.

At the front of their body, scorpions have a pair of huge pincers that are hard and very strong. They use these to hold and crush **prey**. Scorpions also have a large, curved tail with a stinger at the end. The tail can curl forward so the stinger can inject **venom** into animals that attack it or into its prey.

The most venomous scorpion in the United States is the bark scorpion.

"I SURVIVED..."

THIRTY-FOUR-YEAR-OLD STEVE BRADFORD WAS WEARING FLIP-FLOPS WHILE CAMPING IN THE DESERT IN THE UNITED ARAB EMIRATES, WHEN HE STOOD ON A BLACK SCORPION BURIED UNDER THE SAND. THE SCORPION STUNG HIM ON HIS RIGHT ANKLE AND HE WENT INTO SHOCK FOR 10 MINUTES. HE BEGAN VOMITING AND HIS LUNGS FILLED WITH BLOOD, BUT HE MADE IT TO THE HOSPITAL BEFORE FALLING INTO A COMA THAT LASTED THREE DAYS.

Dangers to Humans

Most scorpions are not dangerous to humans because they use their stingers only when they really have to. There are a few species that can be dangerous. Stings from large scorpions hurt, but are not deadly. Smaller scorpions have more venom. Most scorpion stings happen because people stand on the scorpion or do not check their shoes before putting them on.

Do or Die

It is early evening in the desert and you are setting up camp. Your feet are hot. Do you:

a Take off your shoes and go barefoot?

b Put on a pair of flip-flops?

c Keep on your boots?

RATTLESNAKES

Snakes are **cold-blooded** animals, so they need to lie in the sun's heat to get warm enough for their body to function. That is why they are often seen lying on rocks in the sun. Snakes also cope with the dry desert because their watertight skin keeps them from losing too much water.

Rattlesnakes do not hunt humans. They stalk prey that they can eat, such as rats and mice, gophers, small birds, frogs, and sometimes, insects. However, if a rattlesnake is stood on or feels cornered, its instinct is to protect itself. Then, it will dart its head forward quicker than the eye can see, and inject venom into its victim with its sharp fangs.

Snakebite Kit

If a rattlesnake bites someone, they should remain calm and still, and get to the hospital as quickly as possible. When traveling in a desert, it is worth packing a snakebite kit that includes medicines such as an **EpiPen**® that can help to slow or stop allergic reactions to venom.

Do or Die

Just as you jump over a rock along a desert trail, you feel a sharp stab of pain in your leg. You see what looks like a rattlesnake slithering away. Do you:

a Try to catch the snake to identify it?

b Remain calm and still and get to the hospital as quickly as possible?

c Rub your leg and jump around to ease the pain?

Avoiding Trouble

The best way to avoid a snakebite is to stay away from snakes. Look out for snakes all the time. Stay on well-used trails and do not wander off into tall grass, brush, or weeds where rattlesnakes hide. Carry a stick to shake bushes and undergrowth before you walk near them to scare snakes away. If you see a snake, calmly, quickly, and quietly back away from it.

"I SURVIVED..."

WHEN LORRAINE JOHNSONS HEARD THE SOUND OF A RATTLESNAKE SHAKING ITS TAIL, IT WAS TOO LATE. THE 3-FOOT (1 M) SNAKE HAD ALREADY SUNK ITS FANGS INTO HER ANKLE. WITHIN SECONDS, HER VISION WAS BLURRED AND HER LEGS FELT LIKE JELLY. SHE KNEW SHE WOULD LOSE CONSCIOUSNESS SOON. LUCKILY, SHE MANAGED TO STUMBLE TO A ROAD WHERE A PASSING CAR STOPPED AND TOOK HER TO THE HOSPITAL IN TIME TO SAVE HER LIFE.

Keep back! A rattlesnake's strike distance can be one-third to one-half of its overall length.

GILA MONSTERS

Gila monsters are poisonous lizards that can grow up to 2 feet (60 cm) long. They spend most of their time in underground burrows, coming out only to lie in the sun and to feed. They eat mainly baby mammals and eggs that they steal from nests. They store fat in their large tails, so they can go for months without food if they have to.

Gila monsters tend to avoid humans and other large animals, but will attack if they feel threatened. When they bite, they clamp their teeth firmly into their victim. They chew the venom into the skin rather than injecting it through hollow fangs, like a snake. Fortunately, although a Gila monster bite is very painful, there have been no reported human deaths from one.

"I SURVIVED..."

IN JUNE 2008, A 24-YEAR-OLD MAN WALKING IN THE SAGUARO NATIONAL PARK SPOTTED A GILA MONSTER. UNAWARE HOW DANGEROUS IT WAS, HE PICKED IT UP. THE MONSTER BIT HIM ON THE NECK AND HANDS BEFORE LETTING GO. THE MAN WALKED ON, BUT SOON HAD TROUBLE BREATHING AND WAS VOMITING. LUCKILY, HE FOUND SOMEONE TO CALL AN AMBULANCE AND GOT TO THE HOSPITAL IN TIME TO BE TREATED FOR THE BITES, HEAT EXHAUSTION, AND SEVERE DEHYDRATION.

Gila Bites

If a Gila monster bites someone, submerging the Gila monster in water may force it to let go, so the person can escape from its strong jaws. However, there is not a lot of water in deserts, so the best way to avoid a Gila monster bite is to stay away from Gila monsters!

Do or Die

You are in the desert when you spot a Gila monster in the entrance to its burrow. Do you:

a Walk away and leave it alone?

b Sit next to the hole to wait for it to come out?

c Put your hand into the hole to try to pick it up?

The Gila monster is North America's largest lizard.

Chapter Five

NATURAL HAZARDS

Deserts are wild, isolated places where the weather can change quickly, causing a variety of natural hazards. **Floods** can suddenly cover land with gushing water, and **quicksand** can swallow up people. Strong winds can blast sand against the skin, and alter the landscape to confuse people.

Winds happen because of heat. When the sun's warmth reflects off light-colored desert sands, it warms the air above the ground. Warm air rises and cooler air moves in to fill that space. This moving air is wind. Winds can move quickly across deserts because there are few obstacles, such as buildings or hills, to block or slow its movement.

Always check the weather forecast before setting off on a desert adventure.

An Eye on the Sky

The most important thing a person can do before setting off on a desert adventure is to check the weather forecast and find out as much as possible about the place they are going to. If storms or strong winds are forecasted, people may have to change their plans. Although it is a shame to cancel a trip, it is more important to be safe. While travelers are in the desert, they should check the sky for signs of a change in the weather.

Distance Matters

In the desert, people can be far from the hospital or town, so even a minor injury or accident can become serious because it can take so long to get help. If a disaster happens, people should try to make a plan before they take any action.

Desert storms are a problem because they can cause floods and sandstorms.

Do or Die

You check the weather forecast before a desert trip and it says there is a risk of storms. Do you:

a Go ahead with the adventure as planned?

b Take extra supplies?

c Postpone the trip to another week?

SANDSTORMS

In a sandstorm, strong, swirling winds lift the top layer of sand from the ground, and blow it around in all directions. All people can see is a huge, yellow wall of sand, and all they can hear is the roar of the wind. Some sandstorms can reach heights of 3,300 feet (1,000 m) and race along at more than 25 miles per hour (40 kph).

A sandstorm can start suddenly and close in on people quickly. Sandstorms can block out the sky and make it impossible for people to see where they are going. As they stumble around, they may get lost or fall and injure themselves. Fast, windblown sand can sting as it hits bare skin, and can make it very difficult to breathe.

"I SURVIVED..."

In 1994, 39-year-old Mauro Prosperi took part in a six-day race through the Sahara. On the fourth day, a violent sandstorm struck. When it ended eight hours later, it was dark and he was lost. He survived by eating raw snakes, lizards, and bats. He drank his own urine and sucked plant juices for water. Ten days later and 181 miles (291 km) off course, he walked into a Berber camp. He had survived.

What to Do

As soon as someone sees a sandstorm approaching, they should cover their mouth and nose, and run for shelter behind rocks, small trees, or in dried-up stream beds. If people are in a group, they must try to stay together as it is easy to get lost in a sandstorm.

Do or Die

It is a clear-blue day in the desert when suddenly you see a dark yellow wall of sand and it is moving toward you. Do you:

a Pause to take a photograph of the storm?

b Cover your mouth and nose and run for cover?

c Cover your mouth and nose and close your eyes?

Sandstorms occur in desert regions across the world.

QUICKSAND

In movies, quicksand swallows up victims like a hungry monster. In real life, quicksand is not so dramatic, but it can still be dangerous. Quicksand occurs when water flowing underground soaks an area of loose sand above it. The sand moves more like a liquid than a solid, and cannot support any weight.

Quicksand can be dangerous, but luckily most areas of quicksand are only a few feet deep.

One way for people to avoid quicksand is to learn where it happens and walk around it. People should look out for ripple patterns in areas of sand or sand where water is seeping through to the surface. If they are at all concerned, they should push a stick into the sand to check if it is safe before walking on it.

It is not difficult to escape from quicksand if people keep their cool and know what to do.

Do Not Panic!

Quicksand sounds terrifying, but it is easier to escape from than people might think. The important thing is to not panic. If a person steps onto quicksand, they need to remove anything heavy, such as a backpack, which could weigh them down. They should move slowly, even if that means that it takes a long time to escape. If they move too quickly, they will just disturb the quicksand and create more quicksand.

Float Away

Just as humans can float on water, they can also float on quicksand. Most people who die in quicksand do so because they panic and thrash around. The more they struggle, the faster they sink. If people lie back, with their legs together, floating at the surface, they can gently paddle to safety.

Do or Die

You are hiking alone in the desert when suddenly you find yourself trapped in quicksand, sinking fast. Do you:

a Wave your arms about and call for help?

b Lay back and let yourself float on the surface?

c Kick your legs and try to walk to the side?

FLASH FLOODS

In the desert, more people are killed by flash floods than by heat exhaustion or dehydration. A flash flood happens when a sudden, powerful rush of water flows through a river **valley**, **canyon**, or dry riverbed. Flash floods often start when rain falls on a mountain and is funneled down its side. Flash floods can strike without warning, leaving desert hikers and explorers in serious danger.

"I SURVIVED..."

In August 1997, Pancho Quintane was leading 11 hikers down a deep canyon when a flash flood filled the canyon with water 11 feet (3.3 m) high. The 11 hikers were washed away to their deaths. Pancho was tossed around and thrown against the canyon walls before managing to grab a ledge and pull himself out. The force of the water had ripped off all Quintane's clothes and he was badly bruised, but he survived.

You and a group of friends are hiking on a dried-up riverbed when you see storm clouds in the distance. Do you?

a Keep on walking—the storm looks far away?

b Climb out of the riverbed immediately?

c Keep on but check the sky often?

In flash floods, when it is moving quickly, even shallow water can sweep people off their feet.

Flooding happens in desert areas because after long periods with little or no rain, the ground in deserts can become hard and dry. When there is a spell of sudden heavy rain, the water cannot soak into the hard ground quickly, so it flows across the surface. Before heading out into a desert, people should check the weather report for flood warnings.

How to Survive

If a flash flood hits and people are in a valley or on a riverbed, they must move to higher ground as quickly as possible. In an emergency, they should drop any belongings, such as heavy backpacks, which could slow them down. If people are caught in a flood, they should try to grab a tree or ledge to keep themselves from being washed away.

Chapter Six

ESCAPE THE DESERT

When things go wrong and people are stranded in the desert, they need to do all they can to survive and escape as soon as possible. If a jeep has broken down or an airplane has crashed, the best course of action may be to stay with the vehicle. If travelers have told people at home the route they were planning to take, staying with the vehicle offers the best chance of being found.

In a desert, vehicles are larger and much easier to detect than a human from a rescue helicopter. Staying by a vehicle is also a good idea because it contains things that can help people survive, such as shelter and lights. A vehicle also has a horn, which people can use to signal for help.

If a jeep gets stuck in the sand it is sometimes possible to push it out.

Do or Die

Your plane crashes in the desert and you are the only survivor. You are miles from the nearest town. Do you:

a Set off in the direction of the nearest town?

b Look for help in the day but sleep in the plane at night?

c Stay in the aircraft and wait for rescue?

On the Move

If travelers have not told people where and when they are traveling, a search-and-rescue party will not look for them. In that case, the only option may be to leave the vehicle and go in search of help. Before people leave, they should put a note on the vehicle saying what happened and in which direction they have headed.

If an aircraft crash-lands in a desert it is usually safest to stay near the plane and wait for rescue.

Finding Help

If people have decided to leave their vehicle, they should take useful items from it, but not too many to weigh them down. Walking at night is cooler and reduces water loss from sweat, but people will need a flashlight. This will also be useful for signaling at night if a vehicle passes nearby. They should walk slowly to save energy.

LOST?

Getting lost in a desert is frightening. If hikers walk in the wrong direction, they could find themselves even farther away from the nearest town. They could also end up spending longer in the desert and increasing their risk of suffering dehydration, heatstroke, and starvation. Anyone visiting a desert should have the equipment and training they need to **navigate** and find their way out again.

People should never travel to deserts without a map, **compass**, and a GPS device. A map with important **geological features** on it can help people find their way in some deserts. A compass has a needle that always points north, so people can figure out the direction they need to take. GPS devices use satellite links to pinpoint where people are and where they need to go. A cell phone can be useful if there is a signal.

"I SURVIVED..."

IN JANUARY 2009, A ROMANIAN HIKER BECAME LOST FOR SIX DAYS DURING A LONG WALK NEAR ULURU IN THE AUSTRALIAN DESERT. HE RAN OUT OF FOOD AND WATER ON DAY THREE BUT MANAGED TO KEEP GOING. LUCKILY, HE STUMBLED INTO AN AREA WITH CELL PHONE RECEPTION AND WAS ABLE TO USE HIS PHONE TO SEND HIS GPS LOCATION TO HIS PARENTS IN ROMANIA. THEY ALERTED RESCUERS AND HE WAS SAVED.

Using the Sun

Without equipment to help them navigate, people can figure out directions by watching the sun because it rises in the east and sets in the west. If they recognize the stars in the night sky, they can also use those to navigate. When walking, people should walk in one direction to avoid traveling in circles.

Being able to read a map could prevent people from getting lost or help them find their way to safety if they do get lost.

Do or Die

You are stranded in a desert and have no equipment to help you navigate. You know you have to go east. How can you tell which direction is east?

a Watch the sun. It rises in the east.

b Watch the sun. It rises in the west.

c Watch the sun. It rises in the north.

RESCUE!

To be rescued in the desert, people have to make themselves seen. Desert travelers should carry signal flares with them. They can shoot the flares into the sky to alert rescuers. They can use other signals, too. They can use wood to light fires and send smoke into the air. They can use clothing, rocks, or logs to spell out HELP, to be seen from the air.

To send a signal, people can honk the horn of a vehicle or blow a whistle. Instead of blasting a horn or whistle all the time, they should make sound signals in short bursts of three. This is the most common emergency signal. It is recognized as a distress call and will not be mistaken for an animal sound or a stuck horn.

Do or Die

You are in the desert and see a group of hikers walking at some distance away. What sounds should you make to attract their attention?

a Repeat three short blasts of a vehicle horn.

b Put your hand on the horn and keep it blasting.

c Shout as loudly as you can.

Mirror, Mirror

Mirror signals can be seen for miles in a desert. If people do not have a mirror, they could use one from a vehicle or use any reflective surface. To use a mirror, they should angle it toward the rescuers and tilt it slightly back and forth, so it reflects the sun toward them.

Writing SOS in the sand tells rescuers that help is needed.

"I SURVIVED..."

When 64-year-old Ed Rosenthal tried a new route while on one of his favorite hikes in Joshua Tree National Park, California, he became lost for six days. Rosenthal drank his own urine and sucked the moisture from plants, but he became so weak and tired that he wrote his will on his hat. Luckily, sudden rainfall gave him enough water to survive until he was spotted by a helicopter and rescued.

Distress flares can be seen from far away.

BE PREPARED

Deserts can be deadly, but people have a better chance of survival if they are prepared. There is no reason to fear deserts as long as people take precautions to protect themselves and their equipment. As well as planning properly and taking the correct supplies and navigation equipment, being prepared also means learning what to do to survive in case of an emergency.

People need to pack a variety of things including an emergency distress flare, a first aid kit that includes an antivenom pump for scorpion stings and snakebites, and **insect repellent**. They should take the right clothing. This includes a waterproof jacket for rain and a fleece for nighttime. They also need to take more food and water than they think they will need, and salt tablets to replace salts lost through sweating.

Taking Tools

Useful tools to take on a desert trip include a knife, cooking utensils, a flashlight and extra batteries, matches and/or a flint stick, a small spade, a stove, and extra fuel. If planning a trip longer than a day, people should also bring a tent, a ground cloth, and a sleeping bag. It is also important to carry a satellite phone with coverage in remote places.

Help from Nature

People can also find what they need to help them, if they know what to look for. They can get water and food from desert plants and animals. They can make fires from wood for warmth at night and to signal for help. They can shelter in caves and beneath rocky ledges to escape the sun.

When people are well prepared they can relax and enjoy their desert adventure.

Do or Die

You are planning a short afternoon hike in the desert. Do you take:

a Just water and food?

b A basic set of supplies, first aid kit, and a satellite phone?

c Nothing—you will not be gone for long?

ANSWERS

Would you survive if you were on your own and stranded in a desert? Check your answers against these correct ones to see if you know how to survive.

Pages 6–7
Answer: B

It is best to avoid the hottest part of the day to reduce water loss through sweating. You need to get plenty of rest or you will collapse from heat exhaustion.

Pages 8–9
Answer: A

Thin, light, and loose long clothing will cover your skin and keep you cool. Thin, black clothes absorb heat and pass it to your skin. T-shirts and shorts leave too much skin exposed.

Pages 10–11
Answer: B

Deserts are very cold at night and the best option is to stay inside the vehicle because it will give some insulation from the cold.

Pages 12–13
Answer: C

Night falls quickly in a desert, so there is no time to waste. Build a shelter first, and then look for wood if there is enough light. Do not risk walking farther because you may find you have neither shelter nor a fire to keep you warm.

Pages 14–15
Answer: A

It is best to pack long-lasting, high-energy foods that are also light to carry. Food that melts and fresh food that rots quickly in heat are not a good idea. However, if you eat fruit in the first few hours of the trip, it will provide some welcome water.

Pages 16–17
Answer: C

It is vital to replace fluid you lose through sweating and walking, even if you do not feel thirsty. Being thirsty often means that you are already slightly dehydrated.

Pages 18–19
Answer: C

You need to find help and more water, so it is best to eat a small amount of food to give you energy and so that you have some food for later, too.

Pages 20–21
Answer: A

You should never touch or approach insects or other desert animals if you are not certain it is safe to do so. Avoiding encounters with wildlife is one way to be safe in the desert.

44

Pages 22–23

Answer: C

Going barefoot or wearing flip-flops leaves you at risk from stings and bites from the animals lurking just below the sand or among plants.

Pages 24–25

Answer: B

Even if you are not sure what kind of snake bit you, do not waste time. Find someone to take you to the hospital immediately. Do not move around or rub the bite wound because this will just spread the venom faster.

Pages 26–27

Answer: A

Gila monsters are afraid of people. They will not bite unless cornered or picked up, so it's best to leave them alone.

Pages 28–29

Answer: C

If there is any doubt about the safety of a trip, you should cancel it.

Pages 30–31

Answer: B

It is important to cover your face, but you should also try to get to shelter. Sandstorms can last for hours and can be very dangerous.

Pages 32–33

Answer: B

You have to relax and lie back and float on deep quicksand, otherwise you will not escape. Fast movements will just make you sink deeper.

Pages 34-35

Answer: B

Flash floods can happen suddenly so it is never worth taking a risk. Climb out of riverbeds or any channels where water can travel through quickly.

Pages 36–37

Answer: C

The best option is to stay by the airplane at all times. Aircraft follow a specific flight path that people will know and rescuers will follow.

Pages 38–39

Answer: A

The sun rises in the east and sets in the west.

Pages 40–41

Answer: A

You will exhaust yourself by shouting and it is very likely that you will not be heard. A constant car horn sounds like the horn is stuck. Three short bursts of sound is an international emergency signal that rescuers will recognize.

Pages 42–43

Answer: B

Even a short trip into the desert can be dangerous unless you have some basic supplies, a first aid kit, and a satellite phone.

GLOSSARY

adaptations features that help an animal or plant survive in its habitat

adapted suited to an environment or habitat

allergic reactions bad reactions that the body has to a food or substance

bacteria very tiny living things that can cause disease

Berber desert people from North Africa

canyon a deep, rocky valley with steep sides and often a stream or river flowing through it

carbohydrates a type of food that gives people energy when they eat it

cold-blooded having a body temperature that is similar to the temperature of the environment

compass a device with a magnetized pointer that shows the direction of north

dehydrated not having enough water in the body

dormant resting

EpiPen® a device that injects medicine to stop or slow an allergic reaction

evaporation when a liquid turns into a gas

floods large amounts of water covering an area of land that is usually dry

geological features natural features on Earth, such as valleys, canyons, river channels, bays, caves, and cliffs

global positioning system (GPS) a system that helps people find their location on a map

heat exhaustion a condition that occurs when someone has been too active in the heat, making them sweaty, weak, and dizzy

heatstroke a serious condition that occurs when someone gets so hot they stop sweating and collapse

hypothermia a condition in which the body gets too cold to function

insect repellent a spray or liquid that keeps away insects

internal organs body parts found inside the human body, including the lungs and heart

mammals animals with hair on their bodies that can (if female) feed young with milk from their bodies

navigate to find one's way around

predators animals that hunt and eat other animals

prey an animal that is hunted and eaten by other animals

pulse heartbeat

quicksand an area of wet sand into which heavy objects, such as people, can sink

reflect to throw or bend back light or sound

satellite phone a telephone that works using electronic devices high in space that move around Earth

scrub desert plants

symptoms changes in the body that suggest a person has a disease or medical condition

ultraviolet (UV) invisible rays given off by the sun that can harm human skin and eyes

valley a long area of low land usually between two mountains or hills

venom a poison made by some animals

FOR MORE INFORMATION

Books

Cohen, Marina. *Deserts Inside Out* (Ecosystems Inside Out).
St. Catharines, ON: Crabtree Publishing Company, 2014.

Gagne, Tammy. *Desert Ecosystems* (Ecosystems of the World).
North Mankato, MN: Core Library, 2015.

Labrecque, Ellen. *Living in a Desert* (Young Explorer: Places We Live).
Chicago, IL: Raintree, 2016.

Peter, Carsten and Glen Phelan. *Extreme Planet: Carsten Peter's Adventures in Volcanoes, Caves, Canyons, Deserts, and Beyond!*
New York, NY: National Geographic Children's Books, 2015.

Websites

Learn more about deserts, their plants and animals, and more at:
http://kids.nceas.ucsb.edu/biomes/desert.html

To find out more about deserts and how they form go to:
www.onegeology.org/extra/kids/earthprocesses/desertTypes.html

Join Carl the Coati on a Sonoran desert adventure at:
www.desertmuseum.org/kids/oz

Publisher's note to educators and parents: Our editors have carefully reviewed these websites to ensure that they are suitable for students. Many websites change frequently, however, and we cannot guarantee that a site's future contents will continue to meet our high standards of quality and educational value. Be advised that students should be closely supervised whenever they access the Internet.

INDEX